THE TESTIMONY OF THE BONES

GW00357269

THE TESTIMONY OF THE BONES

MÁIRÍN DIAMOND

WIDEAWAKE PRESS
DUBLIN

WIDEAWAKE PRESS
e-mail: wideawake@eircom.net
September 2000

Printed and bound by Colour Books, Dublin.

ISBN 0 9533857 0 1

Special thanks to Philip

Contents

THE TESTIMONY OF THE BONES

THE LIGHT OF LOVE

I

Last Friday noon, I saw a goddess go;
She moved along Clanbrassil Street
Like a swan! A black and ochre cloak
Graced her fine-boned frame; slender feet
Far suppler than the sally rod.
But it was her hair that enchanted me,
Hanging like a satin mantilla
Down to her thighs; profuse and straight
As the plains of Kildare.
Unadorned, but combed
Sedulously; a sunny lustre
Had lingered there; oh if only I owned
Her hair! Such sensuousness! Like silk's
Lovely shimmer in high sunlight. Smooth-paced,
I verged upon her, all moon-dazed,
Whilst I stamped on her shadow like a ghost.
Myriads of highlights blazed in her hair,
A sylvan-scape had been implanted there!
Barks of elder, redwood and red cedar
Were enwoven into her egg-shaped head.
Shades of hazel, bay, birch and golden chestnut
Eclipsed mahogany, copper and maroon.
Umbrageous tones of pheasant and song thrush
Then obfuscated me. A fine cocoon
Of her long locks tossed in the air;
Hennaed fingernails then touched the tresses
Upon her forehead fresh and fair.
Her winged fingers lifted heavenward,
Displaying an ambrosial forest,
All smoked with myrtle, rose and sandalwood.
Her balmy body exuded perfumes
Of lavender, jasmine, rose and wild thyme;
And swiftly dispelled all the traffic fumes.

II

I saw her rise up high in the sky.
       She turned towards me,
          All shining!
In a snowy-white and scarlet garment,
       Mooned and starred.
Pure linen laden with fruit and flowers.
And between her milk-filled breasts, an ardent
Lapis lazuli rested. Then I saw
An aura of alabaster
Emanating from her poised contours,
And I fell down on the ground with awe!
Oh! Oh! What joy! Strings of liquid laughter
Played in my ears, my face was bathed in tears.
Garlands of hyacinths fell from the sky.
The sun sponged up the tears and soon the moon
Ruled my dark moods; and then I heard a sigh
Like the songs of the sea, and a voice
Sang to me:

       'I am Isis, Queen of Heaven.
       Mater Misericordia.
       Zion's daughter. Star of the Sea.
       I dwell beyond the Galaxy.
       The Goddess of the Fruitful Earth.
       Mistress of Life and Death.
       Bestower of Hope and Birth.
       Destroyer of Life and Death.'

I gazed at this Beatific Being,
The essence of etherealness;
A Presence, truly supreme, profound and pure
Nullified my materialness.

Arms out-stretched, I cried:

       'Mother of Plenty!
       Mother of Plenty!
       O! Please free me

From this Valley of Tears!
Weeping and sighing
From noon to night!'

'Hush! Hush! Earthly Daughter,
Be not sad! Be not sad!
Come! Child of Woe.
Come child, come with me
To the Plain of Plenty!
Through great, gentle grasses
Your soul will go
Before you may see
The Place of Serenity.'

Psyche now sang and lilted like the birds
That choired up in that moonlit, sunlit sky.
Soon after, I heard these supernal words:

'Death of the body starts now!
Permit your spirit
To flow out through your nose,
Release the Energy;
Release the Life-force,
Let go now! Let go...'

Then, a great weight fell upon my forehead,
And a force like fire filled my veins;
A light, much brighter than the sun's ray,
Had flared and flared until my soul escaped.

III

Soon, I flowed up to the waiting lady
And rested inside the folds of her cloak.
How we soared skyward, surmounting the cloud.
The stars had switched on their brilliance, and bowed
As we passed. The moon sat in the sunset

As mellow as a sun-soaked apple.
And Iris called out to Isis and said:

'Venus *praises* the Creator!
Venus *mirrors* the Creator!'

We rose up high beyond the sky
Until we stood amidst the Milky Way.
And then, onward we soared towards that star
Which gives us the wide-open eye of day.
Ah more worshipped and sought after, by far
Is he, than any other deity!
For days and nights we moved through Space and Time;
How my soul, still supported by the folds,
Desired to see the Celestial Light.
So great was this wish that I recollect
Only about an ounce of what I saw;
In case my impressions were incorrect
I will not fill you with illusive awe.

Darkness.
Ah yes, there was darkness,
Days and nights of black sameness!

IV

We floated into the Kingdom of Light,
Gently scything our way through long, fragrant grasses,
Quite as smooth and soothing as a dove's down.
My lady greeted the emerald plains,
And how she danced and chanted midst her grains!
She spoke to sparrows and blue butterflies,
She praised the daisies and the dandelions.

Beyond the Plains of Plenty,
A mount of roses and big diamonds blazed.
I had never seen a sight so sublime;
The earth was but an obscure hollow!
We reached the base, and soon began to climb

A pink-tinged path beside a stream:
The slow waters of the Eternal Flow!

True Beauty inebriated me!
Roses and stones inebriated me.
Isis walked through crystalline water
Enriched with a scatter of sapphires,
Great sober-restoring amethysts, pearls
And patches of red in a bed of gold.
Lambs and cows came down from carefree fold,
All festooned in almonds, fruits and snowdrops.
The Virgin chanted: 'Al-le-lu-ia!
O! Praise Him! Praise Him! Al-le-lu-ia!'
We came to the end of our great ascent,
O and there, below us, like a jewel,
                    The Place of Serenity!

                    V

We descended along a sylvan slope
Abounding in ailanthus, olive and oak,
Until we heard eternal choirs
And sweet-voiced children singing hymns.
A profound silence when my lady announced me.
Then all the saints and angels circled around me,
Bedecked with haloed heads and lilied limbs.
They danced and danced to sweet enchanting tunes;
To blasts of brass, violins and bassoons.
Happy shouts and songs of jubilation
Rang out long through every gap and slope.
Nightingales warmly sang in celebration
High upon cedars and cypresses.
The children clasped palm branches in their arms,
And how their hair was wreathed with sweet bay leaves!
Tenors and sopranos now chanted psalms
For all the mortals leading evil lives.
McCormack, Beethoven and Joyce
Had restored their eyes, ears, and voice.

17

I noticed a thousand-petalled lotus spread out
Over a river of rubies and gold!
A seemly peacock stirred in blissful dream,
And shoals of silver salmon swam upstream.
The eagles and owls tossed drupaceous boughs,
Ripe olives and peaches dropped to the ground.
Great fountains rose from rocks of samphires,
And milk-filled lakes, and nectar everywhere!
No need to need, or to achieve success!
No fear of Man, death, sickness or distress!

Sixty-four swans sailed a lily-filled lake.
Mirrored in lucid water, I saw Blake,
Dante and Yeats interchanging stanzas.
By the Rock of Ages, Leonardo
Sat and chatted with Michaelangelo.
Isis and I strolled through a dell of dreams.
I saw souls I had known and loved on earth;
And my grandma smiled at me from a banyan tree:
                    She had time,
                    She had time for Him!
                    She renounced Self
                    And turned towards
                        The Light.

We bathed in the Water of Life.
Then, I saw, hanging amidst healing leaves,
The twelve fruits of the Tree of Life.
And ivy clung to the Tree of Knowledge
That had tempted, and sadly doomed, Adam and Eve;
Therefore, evil, pain, and mystery followed.

Apollo kissed under the mistletoe.
Aestival breezes lovingly sent essence of rose
To beautiful women with wavy hair.
Near still waters, we saw the sage, Plato,
Who was rewarded for Contemplation;
Beside him, Hypatia, her beauty restored.
And across a pond, lying upon vines,

Marx and Joan of Arc were in quiescence,
For they had no need of their deeds or designs.

VI

          Ascending bowery slopes,
We passed the children born of Light and Love.
Soon, I saw the effusive ecstatics,
Virgins, and the devout spouses of Jesus,
Holy Theresa, and Catherine,
Resting beneath les Cheveux de Venus.
They embossed bouquets of pink roses
And the most beautiful perfume breathed
On me, imbuing me with peacefulness.
How I loved this beautiful place!
Impregnated with purple plants:
Biblical figs and hibiscus,
Lovely saffrons, amaranths, and narcissi.
Great gardens of ripe fruit and herbs to entrance
Earthly senses. And the voices
Below in the valley sang on and on,
And I lapsed into a state like sleep
Till I heard my lady gently saying:

          'Wake up! Wake up!
          We must go and see
          The One who sent me!'

VII

We arose to a lofty slope, where
A praying mantis moved in screens of green.
Mary waved to the four Evangelists,
And hailed the Baptist, 'the most perfect man
Born of woman.' I saw five sages,
All gazing into the distance; deeply sad
Prescience dimmed all their faces,

And O! I was afraid, so afraid!

We floated over by the riverside;
        'Mary!' I said,
        'Who are those three figures
        Kneeling by the river,
        Moist eyeballs rolling downward?'

        'Poor Earthly Daughter! You see
        The divinely-inspired Elijah,
        Jeremiah, and Isaiah
            WAITING IN SILENCE.'

A golden eagle flew towards the sun.
I heard the voices of three disciples
Whispering to me, but what did they say?
What did they say?

The Virgin guided me to a sphere, where
A tint of topaz pervaded the air,
And silence hung on every ray of light.
Emeralds effulged from the verdure
And inebriated me.
She greeted One of her own with a kiss;
Meek and hairy, Mary of Magdala
Just sat beside the Lamb of Light and cried for bliss.

Then, a winged child appeared above me,
        Floating within a ring of light!
With flowing tresses like marsh marigolds,
        His limbs outstretched,
And in a low-toned voice he said to me:

        'See the lady in blue,
        She came to release you
        From your dis-ease.
        For She is Salve Regina,
        Mother of the prince of Peace;
        Daughter of seed and water.
        Furnace of earth's fertility;

Cave of Truth, Love and Beauty.
She is the key to Sophia!'

My lady rejoined me and we resumed
Our voyage. Meanwhile, forms and figures loomed
On far horizons like cars that cast light
Upon the sky in the moorland at night.

Oh how my soul now filled with awe!

Willow warblers and golden orioles
On wing around an edifice above.
And lambent torches of light glowed like coals
In the sky; then I saw the eyes of a Dove
Gazing at me. Topaz thickened the air.
We transcended the source of the river,
And I became aware of a Hawk's stare.

VIII

A palace of alabaster
Peered before us,
All shining like glass!
With walls of jasper
And eight gold doors.
Splendent Sun reigned on high,
He sat in a sapphire sky,
Sweeping rays upon the palace
In an outfit of saffron dye.

And just then, there was almost nothing!

A spark shot through the dark and scorched my soul.
I had never been so exposed!
So exposed!
So exposed!
A light much brighter than electric light
Emanated from somewhere;
It effulged like a diamond masked by the night,
Like a diamond...O the glare! The glare!

'Nearer and nearer and nearer to...'

Dazzled by its constant coruscation;
             Full of fear!
             Full of fear!
I could not see beyond what I could see.
Flashes fulgurated furiously
Sending forth an effluence of energy:
             'O soul-consuming fire!
             Ego is exhausted by awe;
Wishing to quench intensity,
And yet is restless with desire.'

'Nearer and nearer and nearer to...'

             'Oh! brilliant blur,
So like the sun behind a thundercloud!
You let your radiance be revealed,
Yet your mystery *is* concealed!'

             'Burst forth brightness,
             Manifest yourself to me!
             Burst forth, burst forth
             And let me see
             Soul's own likeness!'

'Nearer and nearer and nearer to...'

Light coruscated and intensified,
Soon blinding me with solid whiteness. I cried:
'O mighty mask! But you transcend all names!
             Who are you? Who are you?'
But I turned away! I turned away!

Then, moving back into the topaz-tinted sphere,
I heard a susurration in the air;
Too soon, I sank from ecstasy to fear.
'My soul is lost! Who am I?'

And I felt a presence of parched breaths.
A figure floating on a cloud of light;
Three feet of tresses now swept around my soul,
And carried me from sphere to slope, then down
Into the *Plains of Plenty*.

The voice of Isis then whispered to me:

> 'Hush! Hush! Hush!
> Poor Earthly Daughter!
> Be not sad! Be not afraid!
> O be like the sun at noonday!'

'The Sun consumed my wonder-stricken soul,' I cried.

> 'O Child of Woe!
> Please go back to earth
> For your rebirth!
> Light up your soul
> With mirrored Love;
> Beauty below
> Is like above.
> The essence of Heaven
> Lies within.
> *Son amour:*
> *Comme une flamme*
> *Dans votre âme*
> *Toujours*!
> His love
> Like a flame
> In your soul
> Forever!'

THE FLOWER OF LIGHT

I recollect a cool, March afternoon
Rambling Renvyle's peninsula
When terrestrial soul was in tune
With euphonic echoes of energy.
Roused by a Connemara-marbled sea
And a pearl-blue, Connemara sky.
Alone, alive, and *aware* of how free
I felt, far from the judgement of mankind.

Near a pier of shells and pebbles
I trampled on a stony grave of famine bones:
'This should not have been your ossuary!
You humbled Self for God to hear your rabid moans;
Yet he let you linger long in misery!
You combed Renvyle for food, and found no more
Than grass. Thin, febrile fingers clenched the roots
Of earth; you suffered enough, and were heard no more.'

Moving along in a meditative mood;
Slipping away from adultness,
Then slipping back to pristine Bloomhood.
Allowing myself to flow flow flow
Like the sea, like a wave, like the sea.
In rapport with the Atlantic Ocean:
            'Wrapped in your rhythms,
            Co-eternal Ocean!
            Wrapped in your rhythms
            Feeling your motion
            Animating me!'

And I saw a flame upon the water.
Lifting lids I gazed north-westward,
And fixed mortal eyes upon the Fire
Of Eternity. Larger than a star,
Smaller than the sun, it burst through a cloud
Like a flower of topaz. How desire
Took root within psyche, purging out

Carcinomas from earth-bound delusions.
The Gold of Heaven burst forth girded by
An aura of gold, and a golden wand
Pointed seaward. Such beauty! I
Was numb with awe, but filled with love and longed
To levitate:

> And be the image of it,
> Perfect and beautiful!

Soul was in control of its harness,
Galloping round every path of the earth;
Moved by One Celestial Consciousness,
Which laboured to circulate the birth
Of Beauty, Light, and Wisdom within.
Recognising strange, untravelled regions,
Where everyone shared One Intellect;
Forming a universal allegiance.

My body returned to the world of sense,
To a world of sickly sunlight.
I was an airy being, born of love,
That had fallen from that flower above;
                    Fallen
          Fallen
Fallen into the foul, open arms
Of mankind.

And I saw it close like a rose;
Close like a rose in the gloaming!
Drained by an ebbing energy:
          Drained drained drained
What pallid sky! What ugly sea!
What a death-dominated earth!
A hollow of dying people and rotting dead.

'Gold of Heaven, tell me what's the point of birth?'
Just then, it ceased to be.
Cursed consciousness! My thought-worn body
Turned away from truth; and the vision died so.

The sea looked sick, the sky a drained blood bank.
I could still see the afterglow,
And with child-like hope, I prayed:
> 'Ah stay, shining flower!
> Be the Light of Love;
> Shed your thousand petals
> Round this Garden of Nettles!'

I waited long, and lingered on in vain
For signs of proof to please Intellect.
And with newly-purged reality sighed:
> 'Momentous alienation!
> I have seen, and *know* I have seen!
> Millions have seen, but ignore
> It, for they charge Imagination.'

Must I still be a shadow
Clenching the roots of this rank, sombre hollow?
Where soil is ill with seeds of evil deeds,
Where earth might become bankrupt for heirs to follow:
Arms, machines, bombs and bodies built to blast
The earth. A god-conquering modern man!
A devil-damned destroyer of everything
But death! Must I still be a shadow?

And mirrored in lapping water I saw:

> A beauty-queen who walks
> The jewelled ramp of night
> Without an audience.
> 'Lady of beautiful lovers,
> Be the substitute light!
> Come to me in reverie!
> Show me once more how to flow
> Flow flow like the sea,
> Like a wave, like the sea!
> Purify all my poetry
> So that it sings the truth,
> Or still me if you will.
> So that we may live

In the Light of Love,
And be its perfect image.'

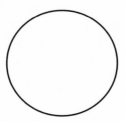

THE BONE FIELD

I

All night long we shed love in the moonlight:
'Ah, Honoria,' said fond Festy,

> 'How how I love you!
> Your flesh: the Food of Life for me.
> Where would I be, my Rose, but for you;
> Where would I be, and you a ram
> After the soul; your Life-hunger
> Dining on Love.
> Hearts that could always sing
> Like the skylark in spring.'

Rough hands roaming me, his tongue
Rousing me out of my reason.
A full moon beaming down on two
Alabaster beauties, alluring me far
Beyond Desire. Mid-month-Fire
Was upon me, and fat Moon herself
Forcefully heaved me higher and higher...
I could have eaten myself with Desire:

> 'O more, more, more Festy more!'

His tongue left an itch in every inch
Of me, but he could never reach the CORE
Where I heavily heaved for more.
Too soon, I'd expect a flame of ecstasy
To feed my fat hunger for Love, for Life,
To lose myself in the soul of my Love,
And find myself like a flower or leaf
In June. We were not born to be in tune
With a beautiful world. Ah, born only to live
For a while, and watch eternal Moon
Show us the majesty of a chestnut tree.
O the sea the sea, the never-ending sea,

Singing songs to us over and over
And over again, ah, but not forever,
Not forever! What were we, my Love
And I, but clumps of clover;
All too soon devoured by the Void of Death.
Myriads throughout Womb of Bloom died
Of It, shall die of It. We lie
Not in rest, and one by one, we will come
And haunt you with awful moans,
Tears and sorrowful tales from a Land of Bones.

II

Memory sparks our midsummer bonfire;
We never laughed or danced for Sun again.
Starry flames and smoke blew higher and higher
Over a firelit, midnight sky
And down into moonlit sea.
A rash of sun could still be seen
Beyond in Cashleen. We knew he
Was aware of our Altar of Fire,
Luring him to linger long in Connemara
Until Hunter's Moon or Halloween.
Then, we would uproot the fruit of the Sun,
And celebrate the Womb of Bloom with fun
And feast. Life was an eternal circle:
Easter sowing; long daylight growing;
Summer of want; winter of plenty.
Fire fed with furze from the Rapefield.
Oak-twig, rag and bone to light
It all night long, till Sun blossomed out
Of the sea, and showed off his mauve cape
To us through his long, fine looking-glass.
We jigged, hopped and jumped about;
Jumping flames, leaping high to make crops grow high.
The joy of lots of infants for the one who wins;
Leaping maidens laughing, old maids sighing.
A bold boy sat upon a burning bush

To prove his love of life to all his friends.
Later, sun-wise we danced, three times, round
John's fire to charm away all harm.
When feverish flames died down we drove
Cattle through ash and ember, charged
Homeward with oak and hazel wands aglow.
Happy as a heart in love, we sang for the Sun,
Threw faggots of fire into fields
Of leafy bloom-flushed luxuriance. Dew
Clung to stems like a necklace of gems:

  'Look at the lovely leaf,
  A bumper lumper
  This autumn surely.'

Dawns later, we took to the slopes of Letter.
Sky-high Sun himself was good to us,
A sign that we could surely hope
To booley till September, feed the sheep
And cattle with a cheap, abounding food so
They'd be fine and fat for the fair.
Ah, there's nothing as nice as mountain air!
Breathing its balmy perfume every day
In the booley; a sea breeze blowing
Heather hither and thither, the land
Below sending us up abundant signs of Sun.
The world was a song, with water flowing
On and on, Mountain-Daughter singing on and on...
Milk spilling over sparkling rock and stone.
Hearts loved the uplifting note of a lark
In moorland air. And we could hear
Moans echoing in rocks and stones: the fear
Of a desperate woman, half-dying in the dark;
Easing out bloody, dung-splashed young.
A balmy breeze blew sweet
Lullabies into booleys, calming
Wives who wore out palms and elbows churning.
Oats and butter clad bones through the blue months,
But poor spalpeens would shoulder spades,
Roaming from Galway to God knows where!

37

Many earned an extra penny airing
Songs and satires on their violins;
They spent all winter wandering from hearth
To hearth dispersing their verses and stories.
We were so eager to stir the silence
Of our souls. Yearning to hear the glories
Of pagan gods and learned lords; since
We were sons and daughters of a land that was once
'A land of our own!' How we had grown
Weary of war and want, how weary!

Thank Danu, we had a hooley outside
Our booley the night before Light
Left our souls! There, we sat without a care,
Watching gunmetal, slow-moving cloud
Blotch a garter-blue sky. The Moon herself
Rose beyond Mweelrea; soon, we saw her fair
Face mirrored in a violet sea.
Moon looking more like a plate of yellow delft
Than a bowl of china! Losing her behind
A coffin-shaped cloud, we drank to the Sun
Instead, he never goes to bed in Cashleen
All June and July. Passing round a whiskey
Jug, we lived for joy, till soon, half-insane
From sun, song, moon and satire, we saw
Herself all wrapped round a jaundiced heap of cloud,
A look of scorn upon her face, a sign
Of future shock. Yet, that night, all slept
In arms of rock, unaware that dawn
Would bear the baby savage that helped
To ravage the root of our sole existence.

III

By Jove, sky above
Nearly tore asunder by noon.
Stunning, bellowing, barrelling thunder
Blasted ears and choked us with fears.

And sky was a forest on fire
Burning clods of clouds, blue leafless branches
Glowed and fell straight to the ground. Earth and air
Echoed long rapid roars, an eerie glare
Crashed into rock and stone, eye and ear
Overwrought with the wonder of flash
And thunder. Pain began as rain
Poured on Man. Had Nature begun to sneer?

Sooty sky. O! I cast a child's eye up a chimney
All day and night until Sun rose a ray!
He was too sick to suck up a drop
Of dew. Suddenly, clay
Was a dripping rag slipping down
Tully Mountain; we fled the booley, stopping
Only to gather sheep and cattle.
The Atlantic was wild and sick near Achill,
Belching frothy foam high over cliff and rock.
Rain softly falling on sodden land. Festy said
In his own sing-song way:
        'God of love,
        There's something wrong above!'

On Garland Sunday: rain rain rain,
And our world was a womb of fog and rain;
Which would finally bring on a labour pain!
Nature invited us to a bilberry
Party on Diamond Hill.
Were we right to ignore the rumour of blight
Breaking out like high fever throughout the land?

I awoke from a dream to hear Bran
Baying at the waning Moon.
My sleeping angels woke as moon-demons
To choke the queer sounds deep in the quiet of night.
Festy fled like a falcon. Fear-lulling three
Angels of Love, I calmly
Moved into the morning. Soon, light

Raindrops fell on flowing waves of copper glory,
Falling on cheeks, which were like two carmine
Roses blooming in a field of lilies.
Ironing out Bran's raven hair, Festy saw the stare
Of fear, which made us aware
Of that queer, dewy, dawn air wrapped in stillness.

'There's a queer looking sneer
Upon Queen of the Sky!
Watch her disappearing
Beyond that awful class
Of a cloud. God be good
To us. Ugh, what the hell
Is that smell, Honoria?'

'"Tis the smell of sickness surely!'

'Maybe 'tis vomit falling
From the sky above.
For the Love of God.'

'It's the fear of God I'm feeling,
That's the foulest smell, my Love,
That ever fell upon the earth!'

A balloon-cloud hung from a maroon
Sky, milky, like mother of pearl;
And my hair rose like wire gauze
From the top of my skull to the tip of my toes.

'Oh, the pota...tta...potatoes!'
Shouted Festy, running like one half-cracked
Into the Food-field of Bountiful Promise.
He sank thigh high into a leafy sea.
Just then, I saw a gust of sodden wind
Lashing the daylights out of the leaves,
And an eternal fog descended on our lives!

Lots of tiny spots blasting blooms.

        'Oooooh you ssssson of a bitch!'

He dug deep into doomed clay,
Grabbed our precious gems:

        'Far gone, far gone!'

We split open, pit by pit, our bite
To eat, our sole life-food; and found
It festering fast in the ground!
We were two gaping gawks struck numb by the sight
Of stinking spuds. Had Sun and Moon defied
Us? 'Where's God? Where is He now?' I groaned;
But prayer was like throwing pennies at the sky!
Shivering leaves withering one by one,
As though an unseen animal had run his breath
Over the blooming surface of the earth.

By noon, the neighbours' lives had nearly stopped
Forever. Sorrow-stooped, the old sat crouched
Upon stone walls like scolded sheepdogs
Gazing at God's grand Will and Love for His people:

        'Father Rooaun is wrong again,
        What sort of God would give us pain!'

        'Do I deserve to die
        In some dark windy ditch?'

        'Maybe 'tis her warning to mend my ways.'

        'I've seen the devil at the end of my days!'

                In the mellow hour, light
Wrapped itself round a shawl of purple fog.
We could hear unseen sobs of howling people

41

Prowling patches of blasted joy and beauty:

'Sure, we're all burnt by the same bloody flame!'

A sewer could not smell as vile or sour
As our dark dark, stark fields of festered food!
Bird and beast called out to eerie earth, appalled
By the queer quietness, and the foul smell
Of her breath. The caw caw caw of the crow,
And the raucous cry of the raven could tell
Us that Earth had just given birth to bitter sorrow.

IV

A false air of hope on Fair Day.
I soaped my darling Daisy
Till she shone like Venus in a moonless sky.
And I would show the world my scarlet frock,
With its lovely, ebony ribbons and bows:

'For Honoria, my heart's flame!
How it flows and flows like blood
Over your milk-brimmed breasts
And down your lovely, limber bones!'

I mantilla-draped hair, and sack-wrapped feet
For fear of spoiling the hour
Spent beautifying my work-worn body.
Gliding down Dandelion Path, I felt as sweet
And sunny as Queen Victoria upon
Her throne! Ah, but I, Honoria, the tenant,
Was only her winter shadow! Sullied
By slush, spits, muck, bits of bog and marsh,
It is no wonder when Beauty tears asunder!

With swearing and squabbling, it was a harsh
Place for an elegant girl fit for a palace.
Sure, I was a lone gazelle lost among
A litter of pigs! I could have come in rags

For all they cared for my ebony bows!
How spirits rose with the noise of hand-slapping
After hours of bargaining and bartering.
Then, the roving-eyed hawk could talk and booze
With the cute old sod from the foot of Letter Hill.

We had the May Eve gale for Noon,
But I had one more mouth in my belly:

> 'Did I wed you to worry
> All my young years away?'

Said I, devil be done with the land, I thought,
And I who was the daughter
Of MacDara McNamara,
Learned poet and landless wanderer,
Who taught a thousand hungry minds to think!

> 'Don't worry, Honoria,'

Mumbled Molly Conneely, stuck four months
In life's big swallow-hole. Fear carved into hope
To see her warm seven, hungry mouths.
Her man, eaten by gangrene,
By far the saddest wake ever seen.
Stolen youth was judged Death's dirtiest deed;
But the dead hero was deaf to it all!

> 'Sure, he'd the strength of Setanta...'
> 'And faith, a fine match for Fionn MacCumhall!'

Wives in a corner, keening and crooning;
His final home was carried shoulder-high
To that overgrown field of ghosts and dried-out bone.

V

We still had a vigil at summer's-end,
Despite the blight. And sodden hearts would slaughter
Black sheep to honour the year's dead:
Gone to the pangs of purgatory.
Ghosts walked the land, and appeared to many.
Death and Life held their rose and lily
Hearts together. Shades of dusk descended,
Bringing out a flood of dancing fairies.
Fear of God was faint when Pooka roamed abroad,
In the guise of a golden eagle, eyes on
Fire - rrram his neck between your knees
And you'd ride him to the outskirts of the moon.
The young brazened shining fairies in their emerald wear.
Bold and beautiful maids threw balls of yarn
Into the bottom of moonlit lime-yards:

    'Who draws my thread?
    Who shall I wed?
    Come forth, future love,
    Let me see your fine face,
    Lit up by the moonshine above!'

Nappie's daughter, lovely Sarah, saw a demon,
And no wonder:

    'Death is near when demons appear.'

Blindfolded, my own all fingered earth and rags.
I saw three corpses, huddled
Together, wrapped round nutshell ash:
One, headless; two, dreadfully warped!

    'The devil damn it girl;
    You're surely rambling,
    Not a damn thing
    Can I see at all at all!'

Fruit, flower and berry
All devoured by the last breath of November;
Not one sorrel, nettle, dock
Nor dandelion escaped the boiling pot.
Pity sent Poor-love to bed half-warm and fed.
Many a mouth I warmed that winter,
Till he took to the road on a dark, cold night,
Spearing potatoes and stealing 'the stolen'.
Desire crawled into hell for a bite
To eat; Festy's tear-pooled eyes saw growling men:
Crawling   scratching   clawing
Wet clay like hungry wolves that happen
To find a huge dinner in a hen-house!

The poor pawned every piece of pleasure for
The price of lasting a few full moons longer:

>   'Huh, what a price to pay
>   For the pangs of hunger!'

Money: a meaningless god to men
Who thrived on the Bountiful Blossoms of Nature,
Or exchanged labour with lord and neighbour.

VI

God, where was Christ that Christmas? With young
Families goin' the road from dawn to dusk.
Festy's knife bled the life out of a fine fat sheep,
Shared it with souls gone half-mad with a hawkish hunger

>   'Devil a bit is there
>   To eat anymore.
>   We've stripped the shore
>   And the land is bare.
>   God! God! I'm sorry
>   For all the blobs on my soul!'

New Year gave birth to a new fear:

'Brodie, they say 'tis as cheap
As rags in a pawnshop.'

'Not a jingle of joy do I own!
Half-dead and bone-lean
After pawning bed and bawneen!
None of us has land nor money,
Maybe it will rain from silver skies!'

'Jesus Christ, Brodie,
That bloody yella male
Would rip your rotten guts
As would a four inch nail!'

'Hunger took a holiday.
Dawn after dawn
The devil damned me!
A stonewall of a stomach
Rocked about...'

     And soon,
Nature, wise, whispered: 'This food is too crude
For bellies and bowels of human beings.'
Thousands crouched in bogs and ditches,
Tired and ashamed of showing nude
Bottoms to rain and wind and waning moon:

'By the devil's mother,
I'm going to live
One way or another!'

'They thought we'd catch death
Like lost lambs that fall down
Into a frosty ditch.'

'Damn all they care for us, the way
We're goin' before us this day,
Worn down to bare bone, without

A stitch to warm us in some windy ditch!'

Although it was as rough as a varicose vein,
Government was humane enough to give us grain:

> ''tis a queer sort of system
> That fills the gombeen's fist
> While we're fasting to death
> With bellies and pockets empty!'

> ''tis the rich man's wisdom!'

Around the first flowers of February,
Pity padded the wallets of the poor:
Cracking men's backs building imaginary roads.
Pauper fought with pauper for fear he'd miss
The chance of an existence of bliss!

> 'Twill be used to fill
> Out the flesh of fellows
> Who've never laid a hand
> On spade nor shovel,
> Never owned nor loved the land.'

March plunged the knife into the poor man's life,
Out went joy and hope forever!
Hauling and harrowing rock till sundown,
As though they had lived a long...long...life since dawn;
Dragging bare soles three miles through the dark,
Yesterday's gruel gone cool in their bellies.
Mark, the crooked-eyed clerk,
Dribbling them out a couple of coppers:

> 'Soul, soul, let me die; I'm sick
> Of this dark land of doom!
> Oooooh to be dust in the Earth's Womb!
> No sorrow, no sickness!
> Ah 'tis as cruel as Christ's crucifixion!'

Connemara: a bridal bed,
Beautifully laden with moon-lustrous linen,
Beneath a blood-petalled cloud of an angry sky.

'"Tis the disgrace of the place!'

Shouted Festy, shocked to see women:

'Bent down,
Chipping and chopping stones,
With dead-eyed children
Tied to their mothers' bones.'

I saw them moving raw limbs
To and fro like bare trees against the snow.
And Molly, dear Mother of God, was there;
She was wearing away like a waning moon.
Her seven Angels of Sorrow
Looking out of sunken sockets:
        ever-glaring   ever-still
           staring   nowhere.

No woman had so much woe!

'Honoria, Honoria,
A lad from Toorena,
'Tis said, is bad with fierce
Famine Fever!'

'Who Festy who sweet Jesus?'

'Jack Joyce's only son
Jesus Mary and Joseph,
He'll dose us all with it
He'll dose us all to death!'

Terror spread its germs up the high-road, down
The low-road, blew through mud and bog-hut, scalp
Ditch and scalpeen. Hunger dined on rumour,
Each guest shook extra salt on her soup,

And a few chose to alter its flavour altogether:

> 'He's dead! He died, they say,
> When Sun was stretching
> His toes above Mweelrea.'

> 'And we all heard him bawling
> His brains out back the road,
> Sending shivers over
> Every sinner's skin.'

Patrick went out with a low tide and a waning moon
The following noon. We gave him to the grave.
The mournful march of moaning uillean pipes
We never heard again. No more farewells,
No more fine wakes nor fancy funerals;
Only sorrow, only sorrow out-lived us all!

> 'John Joe, I fear Jack's far gone,
> Devil a bit but blood and bone,
> And his lad only laid
> Half a moon in the cold clay.'

> 'Faith, a lousy will to leave your father!'

> 'He's gone, gone since dawn,
> Poor devil of a wilting daffodil!'

> 'An awful way to go,
> And he a tower of a man!'

> 'The very best from east to west.'

> 'Sure the poor soul charmed the eye
> Of Galway in his day.'

> 'True for you, Brodie! Life
> Wears us down to Death.
> Death feeds born Beauty
> To the worm in the Earth's Womb.'

Heaven sent me down her sweetest angel
When spring Moon herself was mellowing
Above Mweelrea. I bore Eve's bloody throes
From dawn to dusk before I, like a leaking sewer,
Pushed beautiful, blue-eyes Fionnula out
Into a home of seven sorrows.
Bridie, beside me, for fear I'd bleed my blooming
Life away; it ran like a river in the blood,
For mother knew her art, God rest her heart!
She beat Life into many a proud man's bottom:

      'Oh mother, you eased them
      Out into a Life of Death!'

      'Mama, so cold and dry down there!
      Can you see them twisted
      Like mountain ash by the winds of the world?'

Many say Lovely Sarah and her mother,
Nappie of the Sorrows, blamed each other:

      'Why must I leave?
      I'd love to live.'

Said Lovely Sarah, soon to die
With no moon or star in an April sky:
Poor Nappie of the Sorrows loudly moaned and said:

      'Aaaah Moon, you mocking bitch!
      I gave life to a witch
      Who took love from a wretch;
      Ripped out strands, scratched my hands,
      Hissed, sneered and spat at me,
      Out of bitter spite, she
      Ranted, rolled, raved and roared.'

But Lovely Sarah grieved her losing gift of Life:

> 'You're the cause of my curse,
> Not a penny in your purse.
> Let me live Lord let me live!'

Thrown out of her own hearth by Noon,
Grave-deep in a bog-hole, Nappie crawled about
Beyond in lonely Currywongaun.
No sun to dry her tears, no sea air, no sky;
Worst of all, no-one could ever hear her cry!

> 'Sarah! Sarah! Lovely Sarah!
> How dare you die.
> Come out Sarah! Come out...'

A rosary of lovers drenched her grave with grief;
Looking like drooping willows without a leaf
In June. All May long, we heard the moan
Of a man who was wounded by the moon.
Garlands of primroses, daisies and daffodils
Died above the loveliest flower
Mother Earth had ever grown!

VIII

May's breath lulled our leafless lives.
The sale of a sheep gave Noon his gale:
Only one lamb left on mountain heather;
What would we do in the windy weather?
Moving around our Altar of Fire,
We sang a song for the flowering Sun:

> 'Oh come, sweet summer come!
> Heat languid hearts grown cold
> With fiery fingers and tongue,
> O come, sweet summer come!'

Gay boys and girls gathered gorse and May blooms,
Hurled them over huts to calm away all harm,
Hailed our stock and plots with holy water,
Held Maybush high to the waning Moon,
While we all happily waltzed round the reigning queen.
Marry in May to the devil's daughter;
No, wait until the beautiful, white rose of June
Sends one out all the signs of Eternal Joy!

Noon and Morrow scattered seeds of sorrow
Soon after Sun sucked up the woes of winter.
No words of mine can show you the women wailing;
Wailing...wailing...wailing...
Damn all to dream of but a burnt-down home!
O memory, cursed-clinging memory!
I saw them root my people out like weeds,
Flinging them to the rocks to rot or ever roam.
Hundred of holes turned into hells,
Down down down they went, leaving their lives behind.
That God could watch such sorrow! What sin?
The Pain of BEING had boiled them half insane!

June was always the golden girl of the Sun;
Breathing Beauty into the heart of Life;
Breathing Flame into famine bones;
Breathing down upon the Moon-loved rose.
Gone, gone, I shall never see a chestnut in leaf
Again. I'll never hear the cuckoo nor curlew call!
How Soul loved to watch all the swallows
Come as lightning over a calm, calm sea.
Mountain-Daughter, breath and sea sang Earth's joy for me.
Never, never shall I LIVE IN LOVE again!

Sun got up and put on his gorgeous glare
For midsummer bonfire on the fairgreen;
He blushed maroon over a moonlit sky.
Altars of Fire sparked on every hilltop
Of Connemara; had there ever been
A heartless winter? And who'd want to die

When Life bursts out of blossom, land or leaf?
Billows of hope blew sunward and seaward
From every valley, village and hillslope;
Long laments to the sun, but no laughter!
No laughter...

       'Poor, poor am I!
       Ooooo pity me,
       God, God, great Star
       Of western sky!'

At virgin-time we threw
Faggots of holy fire into gardens
Of leafy, bloom-flushed luxuriance. God's Eye
Blessed our pink and purple dewy blossoms,
Charged Beauty and Bounty into flower
And food. Eternal Rose of the Sky,
O why, why did you close your saffron eye?

Fourteen noons ablaze before the Fire
Of Love left our Womb of Bloom forever!
Thunder and lightning tore through the dark night:
         Rrrumbling...
         Rrroaring...
         Rrraging...
         Rrrolling...
Tumbling round all night long.

Branch after branch fell down before us,
'O God, your Glare could tear our eyes out!'
Flash crash flash bleached my blinking angels.
So near! what fear! My angels full of fear;
All stretched out, crag-bare, palm in palm:

       'I fear 'tis an awful queer
       Sign from the Sun, Honoria;
       God, devil a blob on our souls!
       Yet he'll watch us worming hells

In wretched hills and bog-holes.
Watch us moaning at the Moon,
All alone on mountain heather,
March howling in our ears.
All alone when death nears;
And raven eyes, rock hard
And cold, will flash like gems upon
Young Beauty gone to rag and bone!

Aaah Moon, sour-sweet Moon, Great Mother of Man!
Lingering long behind a sombre cloud:

'Honoria,
My heart's flame, look at our leaves,
Lovelier than ever before.
Here, my Love, are Fruits of Fire,
Milky rose and lilac promise,
Blooming like life in your dark womb!'

'The roots, Festy, the roots!'

'Do you doubt the Moon, my daft one?
A healthy scalp grows healthy hair,
And a fair skin glows from within.'

Rain rain rain rinsed out the rags of Ireland.
Who could booley while Mountain-Daughters
Rushed down to the sea? Drip drop - day
After day - gun-metal grey; no Sun
To drink up dank air and sodden miles
Of sod. And where was Connemara's mountain wear?
Bog-brown, ashen world; sea and sky: all one.

'Let her bathe our lush Life-food,
Let her lash the Fruits of Fire,
Let her lash away all day, so long
As *She* can still the raven's song!'

We watched our Angels of Love, in dream,
Lying with cheeks floral-flushed along the floor.

Bloated Moon lit up my cliff-cast
Alabaster beauties, and Love once more
Flushed out my Soul, and I was a wave,
Ever roaring, never reaching shore.
Moon lifted me higher and higher
Till I became a flame in Festy's fire:

'Honoria Honoria Honoria...'

Nature's Daughter wept, for she was wounded
Once more. I could not stop looking at Mrs Moon,
And soon I was full of her carmine flow;
Aaaah release release when womb-worries go:

'Honoria Honoria Honoria...'

'More more more Festy more!'

IX

Dark dark the day when old Death came to stay.
God's roaring sigh ripped off the roof on high.
Out of darkness came burning crowns,
And into hearts of hell eternal fear:

'Light of God, we love You!
Light of God, we fear You!
Light of God, love us too!'

Heaven flooded us with her tears of pity.
Once again, we heard those Mountain-Daughters
Rushing down to the sea,
O the sea the sea, the never-ending sea!
Connemara: a lake-land forever dribbling
Seaward. Mweelrea's blue mystery-gown had gone grey.
And Benna Beola was a world far far away.

And once again,
A big balloon-cloud hung from a maroon sky.
We thought God was coming out of holy heaven!
All hearts awake, the world asleep.
Not a stir, not a stir, not a murmur of movement;
All living things were aware of the queer air.
All hearts turned skyward; and knowledge, too deep
For language, gnarled the rivers of our Being:

'God!   God!   God!'

Ah, but God was busily selling Love
To the rich when rag-wretched Ireland raged.
Who could foretell the awful sign should soon shroud
The dead. And whose Eternal Hand
Held up that umbrella-like lustre-cloud?
Blood-sky dawn died down into morning's dark anger;
Eyes never saw such awe! That pearl thing gusting
Seaward...seaward...and sky turned bleak and black.
An angry God; what invisible dust-vomit
Dribbled upon Fields of Bountiful promise.
Bloom after bloom blown out like Man to ash.
What queer Being kissed our cursed lives?
And soon, tawny scars broke out into raven rash,
Ahhh, we saw it all again, saw our leaves
And lives withering before our eyes!

'Here's a cluster of health
From our casket of wealth;
No need to plead in vain, Honoria,
For tonight shall light a virgin Moon!'

'Shh Festy, be humble; go
Hail our field with holy water!'

'See, Sun boiling down those bloody clouds;
Tears through darkness to dry our tears,
His love will soon sponge-up your fears,
For God is kind to the happy mind!'

By the mellow hour, a smell as sour
As hot air from a hag's rotten mouth and belly
Stank our souls. It oozed from the bruised flower
All sunlight long. Our hearts of hell
Howled and howled...

      'Darkness to the day of our doom!
      God has no light for paupers,
      We shall be like worms in the Earth's Womb
      Gnawing raw fish and rotten flesh!'

                    Had an unseen
Serpent licked the life out of blooming leaf?
And Sun shone into all the shawl-veiled eyes
That wailed and wailed. Women, arched like willows,
Howled at God, and cursed the clod that bred them.
Hills could hear the children's fearful, desperate cries
When faith of fathers died. And we saw Man's pride
Twisted into that wind-walloped rowan tree posture!

Festy fled a scarecrow-nightmare only
To hear Bran baying his heart out at the lonely
Moon. No dawn birds sang in our valley of song,
No sound from the living; all sensed something wrong
With Earth's womb. Arm in arm, my Love and I,
Deadly dazed, stood like yews at summer-dawn.
Green Ireland of our love-years had gone,
Gone into the roots of our memories!
Festy poured tears over festering fruits;
My man, my own Life's-Love, was down on his knees
Digging up earth like a dog!

      'Ohhhh mocking Queen of the Sky.
      Has that dirty virgin done it again?
      Darkened our summer-hearts with sorrow.
      Drained the last drop of hope
      From our drooping souls. O! O! O!
      Honoria, all joy and beauty have gone.
      Forget holy heaven, hell is here

In this ragged, stinking, queer,
Sinking hole of maggots!'

'Shh Festy, *You*, you live for Love!
It's wrong to blame the Queen of Love,
By her Light, we burn bright all night long.
O Festy, *you*, who sang me the Earth's song;
Tearful, your eyes, when a beautiful sunrise
Taps the beauty that lights within.
Flowing, flaxen hair blowing on mountain heather,
Your oaken punch as fine as Fionn MacCumhal's!
You, rippling your heart to me, and all the jewels
On earth mirrored in your cerulean eyes!'

'Honoria, Honoria, my heart's flame!
I fear God has gone for good!
We, who shone His Light for Him,
Are clutched tight by the Eyes of Darkness.
We, who we like snowdrops in March,
Red roses in June, shall sorrow soon
When the devil's breath will blow us insane;
Never to grace the world of weeds again!'

X

Terror! Terror! Terror took hold when
Cold Mother England abandoned her naughty brats.
'Landlords, self-blinded, must pay for Ireland's decay.'
Merchants, lower than vermin: and Rody Vallely
Was the only red rose that bloomed
And bloomed in a land of wilting lilies,
But what a weed he was within!

'I owe the carrion crow damn all...'

'Sure the pious sinner pretends
We, the poor, are pagans,
And not worth tuppence

To God!'

I remember dark-shawled May and Mona
Like stark sycamores in soft November.
Worn-down faces, wan as a waning moon,
Eyes of lapis lazuli cast into lead and steel.
How life eats away a woman's Glory!
And Sun danced alone upon bleak, black fields
For no-one sang him love-songs anymore!
We saw only the lilac shadow of twilight
Now slowly moving its veil over silent valleys.

To calm our souls by her balmy waters,
Dawn by dawn, we went down by the waves of the sea.
With all the Life still burning in us,
We shed love on the rocks of Trá na mBán.
Fear had gone, for Mid-month Fire was upon me
And the songs of the sea ever-soothing
Our sorrows. We shed our Love with no Moon
At all to look down upon two life-lovers.
Ooooh and what a Woman of Want was I!

'More more more Festy more!'

All my veins hungered for him long after
Festy's lotion quenched his Fire of Emotion.

How long
Can one Dance for Love around the Figure of Death?
For Noon and Morrow
Soon began to scythe our Hearts of Sorrow:

'Clear them out for pasture,
No gain in crop or grain!'

'No money, no mercy!' was written into their souls, and
Shall we ever blot out Rody Vallely's guile?

'Sell on trust, to you, you tramp!'
Yelled he, 'And I am God's slave,

Only fetching farthings for fancy things!'

'We all carry the cross to Calvary;
God has no time for us, Tom.
When you see the devil's men
Dance a noonday jig on money
Sucked out of the dying poor,
One day, you'll say, 'where's God,
Lover of all that's good?'

'Damn all light at all, only night
Shall fall on a dying man's day!'

And in golden-appled autumn again,
Fever chaperoned our famine visitor;
Called on hunger-eaten souls in huts and holes,
And crawled into every rag-rotting skin.
Purple-spotted people spat blood along
The road; saw drunk-thirsty life dragging heels
To its doom: down in a ditch bursting spume
Out of fagged-out bowels:

'The devil take me,
Dry as a summer's blue sky!'

Then, my hurt eyes beheld a forest
Of heart-beating ghosts, all silently
Walking into the winds of winter.
I saw only three Angels of Sorrow
Trailing Molly; all plum and lilac-gummed.
She smiled her heaven-and-hell on me, for she spent her
Last few heartbeats in happy, numb unknowingness.
And a Connemara-marbled sea still sang
Her songs; who was she? but the Moon's mirror,
Lulling Humanity until we die into her Eternity.
And I would watch the parade of the buxom lady,
Moving on azure ramp above Mweelrea.
'Shall my green eyes forever see you rising
O lovely Moon? And shall other eyes
Live and love long, wrapped in all these mauve

Mountain-arms?' thought I, Moon's dying daughter.

XI

A shining big white ship
Sailed on the Waves of Imagination.
Cartloads of Life on roads to Galway;
Galloping out of Sorrow and into a Dream.
Thorn and thistle grew not forlorn, for all
Blew out before Sun kissed away the dew.
The first flowers of the famine - dead, or gone -
Gone to gain some leaves for their naked lives.
How many reached the New World beyond the blue
Horizon? That emerald sod they never saw again!
Hibernia's poor, lost people on board
Purple Victory and Isolde roared: 'Is God insane?'
For sinless eyes had seen the farewell sin:
Dawn by dawn, Ireland's gale and gems of grass set sail.

No heaven's joy at summer's-end,
No wild earth-praise after golden days,
No life left for Life, no life left
For laughter! Only the lonely, awesome
Cry of the Banshee - all the raven hours long -
Combing a lake-rippling of carrot hair
With her silver comb and her fantastic fingers.
But still, on the Hill of Rath, some heard the Song
Of Ireland long ago. Piping fairies,
In starlit green, were seen dancing around a Ring
Of Light. They say wandering hunger saw earth's mirror,
Mary Bride Heanue of the golden hair,
Laughing in dream-love with a haggard king!
The carnage-knived pits had lost their pain,
For eyes flashed upon Beauty in shining wear,
Heaven's window-lit sky grew dim
Watching her robe with a diamond rim.

'Honoria! Honoria! Where's my Lily?
Lily..Lily...my own lovely Lily!'

I had heard the ghost of Molly say:

'Lily went out before the waxing Moon
Shone on the auburn beauty of autumn.
Peace Molly. Peace...
For Lily floats on golden clouds of joy!'

By the light of a blossoming Moon,
Life's true-love and I, wandering the lone highroad,
Walked right into a World of Shadows.
Men raging and soughing at the Moon for death,
And a woman sighing, for her flame was dying.
Earth-ghosts appeared; spectres disappeared; madmen rose;
And we said 'goodnight' to the living and the dead.
The banshee crooning the Song of Sorrow:
All night long bringing death-quakes to O's
And Mac's who lived in the Ditches of Death.
One could hear their last 'Ouu...ouu...ouu...'
On Heather Island. Dark-faced Letter Hill
Was like a black hole in the looking glass.
The deep...the dark...death was pulling us down down
Down... No Love could breathe in the still
Breath of our world's irrevocable LOSS!

November blew in that cold, sharp wind
That came to stay. All gone - the golden earth -
All gone! Half the world trembling
In the arms of Death. From the stony strands
Near Height of Thickets to the golden sands
Of Glassilaun, tree-root hands, red and raw,
Poked pond and rock in long, bitter dim-ray.
Only marble hearts could endure: figures
Bending rag-torn back for hunger.
Black velvet Death came with iron weather,
And flung the autumnal dying like dung
Into an open grave. And human rot

Haunted me till it sank into dank earth;
Foul-sweet flesh on an icy wind blew hard.
All the gale-months long seeds of sorrow blew
Into the essence of soul and sense.
And stench, forever blowing and blotting out
Balmy memories of midsummer magic.
Woman and man were for Beauty born!
Would I ever wade through wafts of woodbine again?
For baneful earth might spew forth sick
Flowers by the waning flush of a wan
Spring Moon. Thorned by thistles of deathly Life,
In vain, I begged:

    'Come, come, O Carmine Rose of June,
    Blow me heaven's balmy breeze at noon!
    Fill my blood with your aroma of Love;
    Come, linger in our souls as brief as we live!
    Man - for beauty born - cannot belong...
    Cannot belong where the Rose forever grows;
    Where Sun on calm seas moves the Soul to song.
    And these mauvy-blue mountains of mine
    Shall go on and on...lit by Moon-lustre's
    Liquid beauty long...long...after I'm gone!'

Who hurled those howling winds across a hungry sea?
Coming out of nightmares with wave and wind
Raging war on land. No joy
For the men who raped the riches of the sea,
For the tough curragh behaved like a toy
Upon the rough, power-waved waters.
Father saw a deluge of Mountain-Daughters
Leaving Ben Baun, they forever fall
Into the lap of lonely Lough Inagh.
Mirrors of God were down in ditches consuming
The half-rotten riches of summer;
When leaves had lost their bloom, they had to dine
And sicken on the milking mycena mushroom.
And who would dare pluck some pleasure
From the pupillary-berried bush

After Samhain? For long-tongued Pooka
Roamed moon-pellucid paths, till desire for sleep
Transported him onto briary cushions.
Only Moon could see him excreting poison
On freshly-licked fruit; and he would creep
Away to the Hill of Rath for the day.
With all the mountain meat long excreted
And October's last yarrow, dock and dandelion,
There was damn all to stew but the dizzy little daisy.

There is no earthly rest for the dispossessed;
They must wait until they flow through heaven's gate.
Will memory ever let go
Of that never-ending wail of woe?
How long had we tilled and toiled the land for tyrants?
Waiting. Waiting...for the grating sound
Of bayonets to slash the silence
Of our souls. And the hard-hearted strangers
On horseback who would strip life's meaning to the ground.
Waiting...

      'Out! Out! Out!
      You rotten, lazy
      Lousy lot, out!'

      'Noooooooo! Noooooooo! Noooooooooo!'

One by one, they dragged them out into the noonday sun;
And in again they went, like bees to honey-scent!
The rough-feeling sheriff shouted:

      'Come out you fly-bitten pig-shit
      Or I'll bore a hole in your swollen bellies!'

      'Noooooooo, ooooooooh noooooooo!'

DAMN DAMN DAMN the sooty souls of the devil's men!
Flame cheeks of crying children
Flung fierce hard against frozen dung.
And a father, choreless for evermore,

Kissed and hugged the doorpost of the past.
True mirrors of the Virgin Mary
Threw their hearts prone; sodden eyes now sad and sore.
Thirsty blood-ribbons throbbing despair,
Lilac mouths lying on slobbery slime;
Hot breath softening frozen sewage.
Aaah but worse than the wind-bites of winter: wives knew
That sorrow-waves would tumble to the coast of time.

'Oh you DARK DARK men! May the Moon
Cast her shadow on you soon,
And may your lives not last
Until the June-day Sun!'

Shepherds could hear the poignant *caoine*
Echoing skylark clear on silent peak
And frozen corrie. Overwrought, I thought
Wailing-woes would wake the dead way back
In the Black Home of the Seven daughters.
And off to their deaths they went with pots and pans.
Dignity dug holes of Shame, and crawled in on hands
And knees. O! Is civilized man a sham? For
No beast-of-kill would do what Man's WILL
Can do to Man! Dark God warmly descended
When the wailing temporarily ended.
No dream-past, nor dream-tomorrow
For the outcast; only the being of Sorrow.

XII

I was the word-songbird,
MacDara McNamara,
from heaven's undisturbed
hills of Connemara.

I remember the dark
of a December dawn,

no heart-lifting lark-song,
only tears of lonely daughters.

For I was their vagabond
father, heir to the earth;
off to the world, though fond
of my home-bond by birth.

My beautiful Honoria!
Mystery's daughter, so like
Deirdre, bent low
in the Waterfall of Sorrow.

And bride, her dewy, sloe-eyed
sister, washed her long, raven
ripples and cheeks of cherry glow
in Honoria's tearful tide.

Limp with love, I walked out
of their world forever!
Though our lives did sever,
I, too, rode Pain about

on a River of Sorrow.
For I took the long road
to death; O dear dark God,
let language lighten my load.

It would shiver the liver
that sharp December morning.
Fierce, cold wind shook the wing
of carrion crow, on hawthorn

limb, stark bare and blowing.
I'd heard only one, long
lonely groan at Greenmount,
for winter's wind lashed me along

With inhuman hurry.
Slow life-shadows met me

on the way to Currywongaun;
half gone out of the World of Sense,

half in a World of Absence.
Eyes-of-azure-skies watched nature
plucking, nipping, sucking
eyes of socketless friends.

I sheltered for a while
to let Soul watch the cool
broken mirror of Kylemore
and its delly delights.

Fabulous Fionn MacCumhall
shed years of his fine manhood
in that ancient oak-wood
by the foot of Doughruagh.

Hung down by long strife and hunger,
deedless, my dead life; in dream,
I was a god-like warrior
in the World of Always-Young.

I stepped out of heaven,
so how can I tell you
about seven God-lit sages
in balmy, bowery beauty.

Nine phantoms of poverty
surrounded me by noon;
Life clouded over
the Sun in my Soul too soon!

'MacDara! MacDara!
Tá ocras orainn!
Still Soul of our time, curse them
all in riverine rhythm and rhyme!'

From sun-sky to moon-sky
it took a fit pair of bare feet

to trod from Toorena
to Torenacoona.

Night of nut-solid stillness.
Night of a thousand streams.
Cold, sharp as a canine;
Moon led me into dreams:

My people, in purple,
laughing in golden fields;
noon-light falling onto
flush valleys and myriad meals.

I dropped out of my dream
into nature's noisy drama:
wind-howl and hammering hail,
birch in the grip of a gale.

Merlin and peregrine
dashing to meet the dawn;
sparrow-hawk in scarlet holly
drunk robin's dripping blood.

Nine rags thawed as I trod
by lonely Lough Inagh;
no threat, nor bout of hell
with a trout in my belly!

Soon, my soul saw the whole
twelve, diamond-sparkling Bens
of the giant, Beola,
buried beneath Ben Baun.

No-one drinks the frothy
milk-falls of her mountains;
Danu, dark and alone
on silver sky-rock, looking down

at her son, the singer
of a thousand sorrows.

How serpentine her raven hair,
wrapped from bosom to bottom bare.

In noonday nap, I saw two
emerald-eyes-of-stone
cutting an opening
in my Soul, but I awoke

to the world all alone!
Foreign, holy fathers fed
the Holy Book to the half-dead
from Recess to Maam Cross.

'Hunger for heaven! Let your Soul
drink the Soup of Salvation!
Let...' A man with his soul on sale
bought the tale of the Second Coming.

God pulled down the curtain
on the drama of day.
Life-death images billowing
in the purple poignancy.

At sun, moon and star-set,
I sat a timeless while
under an old sessile oak
unwithered, but wind-worn.

From crag to crag
two golden eagles flew,
and on his way to the hazel-wood
the bellowing stag.

I dipped Life in a wishing-well
to wash away World-Sorrow,
and on filmy ferns fell
into a night of dreams.

Ah, but I woke to Death
and the World's Eternal Wake!

and the look of the hard
hunger at Oughterard.

'Walk into the workhouse:
sign yourself on for death;
stay out of the workhouse,
or wake up in corpsy clay!'

said a sad old man who had seen
the depths of the Raven River.
His good heart brought me all the way
to the Gaeldom of Galway!

The rot of rural famine
squatted in Eyre Square.
All the squeals and squalor
were more then sanity could bear.

I serpentined my way through
the multitudinous
dying. How grief grew
sow-thistles round my heart!

I spent all sunset
under the Spanish Arch.
Safe in the Past, I let
maggot-memories drop

into a balmy bath
of exotic opulence.
Through the white-maroon light
I could see merry merchants,

selling delicacies,
from the sultry South Seas.
Although I could never catch up
with the moon-in-a-hurry,

I caught sight of Love's delight.
In the music of silence,

in a land without WANT,
a god-like golden warrior

fed on the World's ebony
truth in the eyes of his dark lady;
and she arrayed in a web
of cinnabar silk damask.

I had the Claddagh
to myself when the Sun
stirred the birds to song
and the soul to gladness.

A stranger in danger
was I in old, clannish Claddagh.
I met only frozen
frocks, rags and baby clothes,

which hung above the gutters
like a horde of headless women.
Joining beggar and thief in sin,
I stole for Life at Fish Market.

I sat down with the dead
in a cart at Fair Hill;
saw the living alive in hell!
Soon, Satan and I fled

with a sad society
of Pity and Troubles
far from the sea-airy
City of the Tribes.

In Oranmore, I dropped off
the daughters of Aphrodite:
Two, beautiful, dead teenagers
tangled in each others

long blond hair. Then I rode
four lice-ridden phantoms

to the Poor-Purgatory
in the town of Loughrea.

I slept under a cold sky
of gold and wept away the day.
'Dark Light, you let those daughters die!
Their years of youth lost in clay!'

Ah, but a wanderer's
night-sorrow soon wanes
like the sky-mistress, Moon,
when there is more and more

sorrow tomorrow!
I saw a mother giving
Earth her Sack of Love
by the river Suck;

hunger swallowing worms
that would bite her children's Beauty;
no woman can stop womb's
industry drying to dust!

I tossed bones in a barge
and shook frost from my flesh
all night, moonlight shone
upon the shivery Shannon.

I took a break from Life
on the Hill of Uisneach,
and told a rook on a rock
all the tales of Tuatha Dé Danann.

Soon, I served my belly
a loach at Lough Ennell,
it would heal the hollowing
hell. All at once I fell

into the charms of Ēireann,
emerald light and land

alluring me. I walked
the woods of ash and oak

till swift-footed warriors took
me along Pristine Paths
of Glory. Ah, ah, but the rook
roused me out of reverie,

his caw caw calling me
back to the Shadows.
All day, I could see
sun-dancing daggers and swords,

and bronze-brooched goddesses
in their ornamental dresses
pouring goblets of milk
into the Lake of Love.

Far from the warm breath which blew Renvyle's
ruthless seas, I fed a dying
chorus in the trees. Ten
days marching through towns,

three days in paradise,
dining in rich men's green
and golden pastures; I
gave Sun my stolen sacrifice.

And I lost land and sky
in the Second City;
how could I talk to things
without wings? Mushroom high

felt I, midst mute and mighty stone!
And I, nameless to them, could name
not one unsmiling Life
along the crowded Liffey!

'What made city life so shady?'
I got wise in Watling Street,

I asked a fine lady,
and she cooled me with worldly coldness.

Under a lone, faraway star
in a never-dark sky,
I laid my buzzing brain
down in Marrowbone Lane.

I yawned awake at dawn
in a lake-yard of slime.
Paupers stretched prone, muttering
their grievances to the gutter!

The Sun increased the strength
of beast and human excrement.
I saw a death-delirious
Love-couple having sex

in their marriage-bed: manure!
Soon, bottle-breaking brawls began
when a man came out of the poor
paradise of alcohol.

I saw the dim glow of Death
from the Liffey to Pimlico;
saw the rich glow of Life
too, from lush Dodder-land

to Beggar's Bush. Perfume
and cigar aromas
flowing from 'life-loving' parlours,
human rot from the rooms

of the wretched! One day,
high on the Street of Bride,
I had Sorrow at my side,
and faraway hills before me.

I slept with a cold
fire of old fever-flesh

till a ferocious frost
bit our bony bodies

wide-awake in Stoneybatter.
And, from owl to lark-hour long,
the world passed us by wobbling
through the cobble streets.

I heard a dying man sigh:
'Moon will turn cold on Man,
for he has sold his Life
to the industry of money-lust.'

But a wanderer's world goes on.
By sunset coach, Pity
took me, wan as a storm-slashed sea,
far from slummers' fair, sumptuous city.

The New Year Moon looked down
on mountains of mourning;
for the first time, felt forlorn
in the Beauty where I was born!

Silence threatened to push
Soul down the throat of night.
World stopped still...until I could see
down to the Inward Light.

After Nature had her rest,
crows ripped a rushing
sky of rose, then, dropped fast
to feast on a dead man's chest.

Chewing a limb of lamb
under a howling hawthorn,
said I, 'how are you so hardy
while I'm winter-worn and raw?'

I could have walked away
from myself that nightful day:

itching, retching, twitching;
pain. Unstoppable pain...

...pain was painting pictures in my brain.
Did I ever have Life again?
For I rode the Red Wave
till I turned towards the grave.

Above the snoring bogs
of Barnaheskabaunia, Danu,
bare, on icy Ben Baun, flashed
emerald on blood-soaked sky at dawn.

Familiar voices filled
heath and hill, but could not fill
the VOID in me! A chorus
roared: 'Christ! It's MacDara

back with the weight of the world!
Rest! Rest MacDara! Rest,
or you'll be worn-out wandering
into the winds of the West!'

I dared not stop, for Soul
was galloping to a standstill.
My sloe-eyed, lovely bride
had died against her Woman-Will!

Honoria, my Feminine Core,
still stirred her leaves of loveliness.
'Helena's heart - Honoria -
do not shed your Flaming Glory!'

'No more Honoria!
Without me, may you be
like the hawthorn's milky boughs,
waking winter-hearts to beauty!'

I had all the world to myself
between awesome Doughruagh

and Altnagaignera.
There, by a lone, lost lake,

I struggled to unlock
the grip of Regret; but lost
the Present; for images
of Past grew strong; then grew dim .

And I rode the Red Wave
till I turned towards the grave.
I saw the last moon-glory
gliding above Mweelrea,

the last sun-flame sliding
into the sea...and I
let reality drown
in golden, blue Atlantic Sea.

I saw the Red Wave wash
the City of the Sea.
Noon, eternal noon! No star,
sun or moon ever shone

on shining City of the Sea.
I looked into myriad eyes:
Emeralds and sapphires
in plaster of alabaster.

Who were the Golden beings floating
along streets of pearl?
Plague-free, never cold, never old,
never caught in Life's passing whirl-wind!

Blissful Beings flowing out of great
castles of gold on marble rocks.
Serene. Serene. Too late,
I had seen a world far brighter

than the Sun! And just then,
the Cold Eye of the raven

called me back to the Shadows,
'where am I? Oooooh no! Noooo!'

I returned to Pain,
and World's Dark, Lonely Lane.
I looked for Light, but saw
only sombre sea, and sooty sky.

'Which world is real? The Red Wave
or the ravens overhead?'
I had found the Beauty within.
Too late, I found Light and lost the world.

XIII

Did Daddy take a short cut to heaven?
Why was the poet-wanderer hurrying back
From the world beyond the hill? - to me - no!
For I saw him only in dreams again,
Floating along a Mystic Track
In blazing clouds of gold and carmine glow.
Father! Father! How far into Life's Pain
Were we! All alone in one's own Pain.
Most men fell like fallen trees, but Bride,
Mistress of Birth, tried to master Death.

I ate a meal of moments at the Feast of Time.
Sleep, I would postpone till six feet deep.
Nightly, I let all the Waves of the World
Wash over me; who wants to steep
In a woman's woe? And I would look
Far far into the Carmine Rose of June:
'Mirror of my Soul, give me more and more!
Breathe your Life into each dying pore,
For we shall soon be victims of the vicious Moon;
Mirror of my Soul, give me more and more!'
Air: blade-sharp, and cold as a dead-man's blood,

From where did it come?...from the mouth of God?
I could hear the hoar-bitten dying roar
Above the hurricanes: 'Ah! Oh! Ah! Oh!...'
Vicious Moon shone her Light on virgin-snow,
There was no night without, no Light within.
I saw men with only a yawn
To warm them until a magenta dawn.
Rags of worn-out warmth sailing
Skyward in a gale; limbs that were once
Lovely, now leafless like December's golden rain.
And their women ever-wailing
The wasteful harvests of the womb.
Why is parents' Pleasure born to so much Pain?
Storm-blown children dripping snow
Like the heavenly-falling purity
Of the hawthorn. I saw through the world.
Sea-drenched mothers were surreptitiously
Flung against wave-washed rocks at dawn,
While others were caught in the lure of the sea.
Stark-raving wretches munched imaginary fish,
And a woman gave herself to a surging wave.

One snowdrop slowly popped its head
Up into a dead spring. The breath
Of beauty flowed into my stagnant pool.
Rippling it with joy: 'Stay,' said I,
'Stay', but the lungs of Satan blew its loveliness
Away. O where were the springs of Bloomhood?
Nature-girl Eternal! How I could LIVE,
Dancing days away through daisies and daffodils,
Charging like a gazelle in ever-changing hills;
Keeping in tune with the songs of the sea,
O the sea the sea, the never-ending sea,
Singing songs to us over and over
And over again, ah, but not forever...
Looking into Soul's mirror, I was unaware
Of the truth: that the world, not I,
Would always be there!

XIV

Only God's money could have pulled
Us out of the swallow-hole of hunger.
Festy's quick fist failed to rip through the vile
Rody Vallely's predatory veil:

'Sell on trust, to you, you guster!'

Yelled Rody Vallaley,

'And I'm God's dust,
Nearly blown into the poorhouse
Through Pity and Piety.'

'Pity, you're a mean man surely!
As soon as harvest Moon
Comes round, I'll pay you, you rogue!'

'No way! Crows will have your eyes
Torn out by midsummer moonrise.'

For months, money-free under a cold Moon;
We sold our goods and bought our Freedom.
We were Weeds of Women in the Woods of Plenty
Roving sun-starved paths until the raven
Hour. When the Light of Hope grew dim,
Sparks from the Fire of Preservation
Kept us warm.

Hope stopped. Sore sore were the wounds of SORROW.
World whispered to us:

'We would never again
Sever from One Soul of Silence.'

But where did the Music of Man go?
It died with WILL in chasms of CARE.

Two Friends of Light came to Renvyle
To calm every Child of DESPAIR:
Heavenly-wise Rosamunda, and Aaron
Of the sunset eyes. A sign of God when
They blew in like a balmy breeze in May:

'...They are pouring their riches
Into a soup kitchen,
But for all the love
In the world, I won't go!'

Neither would I;
All youth long I was proud enough to parade
The Majesty of Imagination.
They would queue till the Sun went blue
For a can of soup today, and contagion
Tomorrow. The joy of invisible
Vermin carousing from blood to blood.
Mirrors of whom? Is the overwhelming
Fate of proud humanity MISERY?
A flock of broken beings going to sticks;
Life that was once in the Realm of Oak and Elm.

XV

Not a stir, not a stir from the world, but the sea
Sending spray to the sky; a whirl of power
Blasting ashen air with waves of pearl.
Mad Moon vomiting vengeance over our
Homes; we shook Faith, but not a stir from God!
Ahhh the pangs of survival! The world: eternal.
Man's life: a brief whirl! Each new victim
Of leafelss Life would be Nature's victory.
Grievously tired, sodden, cold and sad,
We fled far from the visiting flood.
Still; still...as trees on midsummer's day
Were the ballooning black and yellow beings.
Unloved Sun shone, but night went on and on,

For when one walks with Sorrow, there is no tomorrow.

The Sun's aura
Glowed all round the heart of Rosamunda.
God's lily-white lady had come to lighten
The Land of Shadows; her good heart was pouring
Love-soup into the marrows of the poor.
Eyes that lovingly sang: 'Live, come,
Follow the myriad Line of Hope!' What scum
Stank there because of the rich man's sewer.
Summer's earth-blossoms had all gone languid and sour.

'America! America!'

We heard World-chorus call.

'Nothing but death can sing
In this air of despair.
Does God love us as well
As does the Angel of hell?'

How we loved the rotting sod of Bloomhood,
Still there after years of care! Sad the dawn
Of farewell without a Feast of Departure.
Not a Womb of Bloom, but a Tomb of Doom.
Not a song in the sky, but the caw of the crow.
Sharp as a witch's tooth and tongue the breath of spring.
Cold rippling underneath the robin's wing.
On left-behind hearts a rock of great Sorrow:
When they went...Old Ireland sailed with them,
Leaving weepers to bathe in a lingering death.

'Honoria, Honoria,
Breathe joy that my lost brother
Is not lost in the bed of the sea!'

And I read:

'Sea and sky, storm and rain
Drove the sick half-insane.

Cold as a donkey's dead
Eye, the straw-soggy bed
On Isolde. They drank water
That would damn the devil's daughter!
God gifted some with a rock
Of a brain to sail without stock.
A bellyful of brine
Turned into mortal wine.
Weeds of the world were cursed
With belladonna-thirst;
A dog's death; and after
Life they heard the mermaid's laughter.
Left to rot in the sea's lotion
They became Eternal Motion.
The dying flushed cerise
Lying in a daze of disease,
Like yews in a graveyard....*still*.
No longer had the will
To wail breath's end. Reeking rot clung
To clawing wretches; on my tongue
Sweat and dung. Soul of the Sea, how vast
Was she, one rolling surge: MY PAST!
We were the Children of Toil,
Lir's lonely swans on the waters of Moyle.'

XVI

Autumn's howl was hell at sea. Winter stopped
Tears from falling on dew. No escape
Till time would fully drape the April fields
And newly dress the chestnut crown. Death dropped
In on us, took Love by the hand to the landscape
Beyond the sky. Poor poor Packie! Death heals
Life's pain; and all the Love of Life poured
Into him in vain! I roared and roared
My last rage, loud and long into Nature's song:

'Blow back to me soon,

83

O my son my son...'

Only wind answered under a waning moon.
Ellie and Annie burning in scarlet flame;
Happy blooms of blissful passion turning
Into the barren beauty of old age.
All the held-back years of tears flowed
For Fionnula, fast shedding her first leaf of life.
Eyes that mirrored paradise for Earth's Daughter
Now mirrored the look of a mid-wife toad.

Still...still...the night a raven that ravaged the Will.
Hosts of life-eaten ghosts in the graveyard
Celebrating the Ceremony of Death.
Awaiting Sun, alone on the hail-hammered hill,
A moaning man begged the Moon for money.
Everywhere I glanced, saw the stare of the Evil
Eye. And following the moonrise, the
Ebony eyes of the Wise Old Woman.
At purple evening, over auburn land,
Sombre smoke hung low like flesh in Fire-Eternal.
Slow hearts worming their way to the huts of warmth,
All waiting for heaven, hand in hand.
So still. The withering Will couldn't stir
The dead. Cold breaths cooling watery fire.
Soul's laughter came soon after Death of Desire.

XVII

'Even the cold heart of Nature
Cannot stop a woman
Plucking the Flower of her Womb.
Honoria, my heart's flame,
Come home before sky-mistress wanes!'

Sang he, like a dirge in the moonlit air.
Seven hours labouring Love on moonlit mountain.

Distress increasing, and a full Moon rising.
Did God get it wrong? What Woman must bear
Just to bring Life into World-Care!
Near the booley, I let myself dilate
Like a vase-embosomed tulip invisibly
Opening. Waters running into Mountain-Daughters.
Cursed with the weight of an iron plate,
My belly could have burst. Under hawthorn,
I counted seven hundred stars in the sky;
Letting imagination flow from star to star
With each new throe. A son of Light was born
For beauty, but would take a million
Of my lifetimes to die. Reaching far
Far into golden eyes, till I could push
Pain away from me, and out into
The world. His cry, weak as a wounded crow,
I knew then all I'd ever he was a Woman in PAIN!

> 'What have you done
> To me, my son my son!'

I was a rushing ravine of carmine flow;
Moon shone the answer: Moon cast a sour glance
On Nature's Daughter. I soon felt as low
As the Sun when he is going into a trance
In a December sky. Lord, I was leafless, with a
Sapphire baby before the fullness of May!
My alabaster beauties had Life
Sucked out of them like two castaway
Milking mycena mushrooms. Bleeding to slow
Death, I watched life soon leave my only son:

> 'Oh Festus, Festus! Your brief,
> Sun-starved Life
> Would be worse than the sweet
> Chestnut which could not leaf!'

Soul was looking into a mauve Moon
Bleeding. My heart drowned in a deluge of grief.
Would I see Life's-Love and Angels of Sorrow above?

Soul would never see the Carmine Rose of June.
Skin would never feel a balmy breeze again!
Music murmuring with a mermaid in calm sea,
O the sea the sea, the never-ending sea,
Singing songs to us over and over
And over again, ah, but not forever,
Not forever! I was a Woman in Sorrow
With the wonders of BEING.

    'I should have dwelt in the Eternal Glow;
    Too late to see the world from within!
    For what all that suffering and suffocating
    In the mire of desire?
    Let the devil damn it all! I AM
    I AM I AM I AM I AM...'

XVIII

There are only ashes left
Of a man when his heart's flame dies.
Her Soul's Laughter could lift
Me out of my Soul of Sighs

    'My lovely Honoria
    Is no more! No more!'

What's to gain with Soul's Beauty gone?
Heart deafens one with an endless roar.
Only the blood of the Moon
Could come out of the White Rose of June.
Hell was there on that howling hill.
Sharp is Life's pain. Only Death
Can heal a burnt-out Will.
I covered my Love and son, high above
Man's worldy sigh; where she would forever
Hear the lark in the sparkling air.
Up where the rainy westerlies wear
And slap the rocky slope.

Where she could see Moon ever-waking up
Under cloud to the sky!
And Sun ever-slipping deep
Into his Atlantic sleep.

'Oooo...Honoria is GONE!
No more Honoria!
Who will light the Fire in my Soul?
God turned the Darkness on
And I will turn it off...off...off...
I will come back as a bull
And pux the whole world!'

Death took hold in the cold corrie:

'Not sorry...not sorry...not sorry...'

CONNEMARA

Wonderful Connemara,
Land of enchanting beauty!
The Twelve Pins veiled in blue.
It's so blissful to see
Such a turquoise sea
Trembling before me; so
Like a bridemaid's bodice
Fringed with Irish lace,
And sequins sown on every
Ripple of the sea.

The sea says, 'hush! ssh! hush! sh!'
In this hilly, silent place;
Hear nymphs whisper symphonies
In the cadence of a breeze!

A land of furze and ferns,
Unsheared as mountain rams;
Sterile soil yields black-faced lambs.
Raw rock wasting in layers,
Quilted quartz frayed by rain.
Terrains of lazy beds retain
The tears of famine years.
Foothills of cabin walls remain
Tainted by fatal fevers
And the curse of hungry tenants.

Stones and bogs in Currywongaun,
Long-boned men are bent down,
Carrying bags all day long
On bare backs burnt brown.

I return to childhood
And the Benna Beola;
Streams of memories flood
My adulthood. The blue

Suit of Mweelrea, across the bay,
Saluted us every day;
We played 'enemies' with friends
Pretending we were men at war.
How spontaneous our existence
Rambling the paths of innocence!

I behold my birthplace
Below in a hollow,
A haven in my Bloomhood;
Beyond its precincts I DIDN'T KNOW!

Tully village was a city,
The only valley in the universe.
Down in my Wood of Dreams
I set imagination free.
My leafy bed upon a tree:
My incubator for reverie.
Wrapped in blankets of blithesomeness,
Rehearsing the roles of adultness,
I was mistress of my mind;
And time's gnawing jaws were kind.

1983

GLOSSARY

Ben Bán: the White Mountain, the highest of the Twelve Bens in
        Connaught

The Booley: an upland summer cattle pasture.

Caoine: a lamenting. It rhymes with *queen-a*.

Danu: the ancient Irish Mother-goddess.

Gombeen: a money-lender.

Mweelrea: the highest mountain in Connaught. Rhymes with
        um-wheel ray.

Pooka: the king of the fairies. Cf Shakespeare's Puck.

Pux: lit. to butt with horns. A fairy blow.

Samhain: the Irish festival of the dead. Rhymes with *noun*.

Spalpeen: a migratory agricultural worker.

Tá ocras orainn: 'We are hungry.'(Gaelic)

Trá na mBán: The Woman's Beach. Rhymes with *sauna gone*.